PRINCEWILL LAGANG

The Social Entrepreneur's Guide to Impact

Contents

1

The Social Entrepreneur's Guide to Impact

In the heart of a bustling metropolis, where the relentless city rhythms collide with the timeless pursuit of meaning, a story of purposeful endeavor begins. It is a story that unfolds at the intersection of business acumen and altruism, where the relentless pursuit of profit meets the unyielding desire to make a difference in the world. This is the story of the social entrepreneur, a visionary force for change in a world teeming with challenges and opportunities.

As we embark on our journey through the pages of "The Social Entrepreneur's Guide to Impact," we step into a realm of innovation, resilience, and unwavering commitment. This guide is not just a collection of strategies and tactics; it is a call to action, a manifesto for those who refuse to accept the status quo and instead, seek to reimagine the future.

The Rise of Social Entrepreneurship

The 21st century has ushered in a new era, one where the borders between the for-profit and non-profit sectors blur, and social entrepreneurs emerge as the catalysts for change. Gone are the days when traditional businesses focused solely on profit margins and corporate giants only measured success by financial growth. Today, a growing breed of entrepreneurs is striving for something more profound, for impact that transcends balance sheets.

Social entrepreneurship, a movement that marries the tenets of business and philanthropy, has risen to prominence. It represents a powerful fusion of innovation and compassion, where entrepreneurial zeal becomes a vehicle for addressing society's most pressing challenges. The social entrepreneur is a pioneer of positive change, driven by an unshakable belief that business can be a force for good.

The Essence of Social Entrepreneurship

At its core, social entrepreneurship is an extraordinary pursuit rooted in a deep understanding of the interconnectedness of the global community. It acknowledges that challenges such as poverty, environmental degradation, and access to education are not isolated issues but threads in the intricate tapestry of the human experience. Social entrepreneurs see opportunities where others see obstacles and envision a world where problems are opportunities in disguise.

The essence of social entrepreneurship goes beyond idealism; it is firmly grounded in pragmatism. Social entrepreneurs understand that lasting impact requires sustainable solutions, and that, often, the greatest change arises from the combination of empathy, innovation, and a resilient entrepreneurial spirit.

The Guiding Principles

To navigate the complex terrain of social entrepreneurship and harness its transformative potential, this guide offers a set of guiding principles:

1. Purpose-Driven Innovation: Social entrepreneurs must continuously innovate, seeking novel approaches to address pressing issues. These innovations are guided by a purpose that transcends personal gain.

2. Resilience and Adaptability: The path of a social entrepreneur is fraught with challenges and setbacks. Resilience, adaptability, and the ability to learn from failure are essential traits.

3. Impact Measurement: Social entrepreneurs are committed to measuring their impact, not only in terms of profit but also in terms of the positive change they bring to communities and the environment.

4. Collaboration: Solving complex societal problems often requires working with a network of like-minded individuals, organizations, and stakeholders. Collaboration is a cornerstone of social entrepreneurship.

5. Sustainable Business Models: To create lasting change, social enterprises must develop sustainable business models that can thrive in the long term.

6. Ethical Leadership: Ethical leadership is non-negotiable in the realm of social entrepreneurship. Transparency, integrity, and a commitment to ethical practices are the cornerstones of success.

Your Journey Begins

As you delve deeper into the pages of this guide, you will embark on a transformative journey, one that will challenge your preconceptions and inspire you to become a catalyst for change. This guide will equip you with the knowledge, tools, and mindset necessary to navigate the complex terrain of social entrepreneurship.

The path ahead may be arduous, but it is a path illuminated by the promise of a better future for all. In the chapters that follow, we will explore the essential components of social entrepreneurship, from idea inception to sustainable growth, offering practical insights, case studies, and real-world examples to inspire and guide you.

Welcome to "The Social Entrepreneur's Guide to Impact." Together, we will explore the uncharted territories of social entrepreneurship, where dreams of change transform into tangible realities. It is here that you will discover your capacity to make a lasting impact on the world, where your entrepreneurial spirit becomes a force for good, and where, in the pursuit of purpose, you redefine success itself.

2

The Evolution of Social Entrepreneurship

In our exploration of "The Social Entrepreneur's Guide to Impact," we continue our journey through the dynamic landscape of social entrepreneurship. Having laid the foundation in Chapter 1, we now turn our attention to the historical evolution of this transformative movement. Understanding the roots and evolution of social entrepreneurship provides valuable insights into its present state and its potential for the future.

A Historical Perspective

The concept of social entrepreneurship is not a recent phenomenon. It has deep historical roots, stretching back centuries. Throughout history, individuals and organizations have sought to address social issues and promote positive change. However, it wasn't until the latter part of the 20th century that the term "social entrepreneurship" gained prominence.

Early Precursors

Religious and Philanthropic Movements: Many early examples of social entrepreneurship can be traced back to religious and philanthropic movements.

For instance, the establishment of religious charities and missions aimed to alleviate suffering and improve the lives of the less fortunate. These initiatives laid the groundwork for modern social enterprises, which similarly seek to create a positive impact.

Cooperative Movements: The cooperative movement, which gained momentum in the 19th century, emphasized community-based ownership and economic self-sufficiency. These early cooperatives, rooted in social values, contributed to the development of business models that would later be recognized as social enterprises.

Social Reforms: The Industrial Revolution brought about significant social and economic changes, which led to a greater emphasis on social reforms. Visionaries like Robert Owen, a Welsh industrialist and social reformer, advocated for workers' rights and the creation of more equitable and socially responsible business practices.

The Modern Era

The late 20th century saw the emergence of what we now recognize as contemporary social entrepreneurship. This period marked a shift from purely charity-based approaches to more business-like, sustainable solutions to social problems. Several key developments contributed to the growth of social entrepreneurship during this time:

Ashoka: Founded in 1980 by Bill Drayton, Ashoka was one of the pioneering organizations in the field of social entrepreneurship. Ashoka's mission is to identify and support leading social entrepreneurs who have innovative solutions to pressing social challenges. It played a pivotal role in popularizing the concept and creating a global network of changemakers.

Microfinance: Innovations in microfinance, exemplified by the work of Muhammad Yunus and the Grameen Bank, demonstrated how business principles could be harnessed to empower impoverished communities. Microfinance institutions provided small loans to low-income individuals, enabling them to start or expand small businesses, breaking the cycle of poverty.

Hybrid Models: The emergence of hybrid models, such as benefit corporations (B Corps), allowed businesses to pursue social and environmental goals alongside profit. These legal structures offered a new way to balance financial sustainability with a commitment to social impact.

The 21st Century Landscape

In the 21st century, social entrepreneurship has continued to evolve and flourish. This era has witnessed the convergence of technology, global interconnectedness, and an increasing awareness of social and environmental challenges. Some notable trends and developments include:

Tech for Good: Technology has become a powerful tool for social entrepreneurs. The rise of social enterprises leveraging digital platforms and data analytics has transformed the way social issues are addressed, from healthcare to education to environmental conservation.

Impact Investing: The field of impact investing has gained traction, with investors seeking both financial returns and social impact. Impact investors provide capital to social enterprises, aligning their investments with their values.

Policy and Advocacy: Governments and international organizations have recognized the potential of social entrepreneurship to drive positive change. Policies, incentives, and initiatives have been put in place to support and promote social entrepreneurship on a global scale.

The Path Forward

As we reflect on the historical evolution of social entrepreneurship, it becomes evident that this movement has deep and enduring roots. Its history is a testament to the human capacity to drive change, to innovate in the face of complex challenges, and to combine the principles of business with a profound sense of purpose.

In the chapters that follow, we will delve deeper into the practical aspects of social entrepreneurship. We will explore the process of identifying social issues, developing innovative solutions, and creating sustainable business models that generate lasting impact. This guide is not merely a history lesson; it is a blueprint for action. It's a guide that empowers you to shape the future, building upon the legacy of social entrepreneurs who came before you, and contributing to a world where positive change is not only possible but inevitable.

3

Identifying Social Issues and Uncovering Opportunities

In the ever-evolving landscape of social entrepreneurship, the journey begins with a profound understanding of the social issues that need addressing. In "The Social Entrepreneur's Guide to Impact," we turn our attention to Chapter 3, where we embark on the crucial step of identifying these challenges and uncovering opportunities for meaningful change.

The Power of Problem Identification

Social entrepreneurs are, first and foremost, problem solvers. They possess a keen ability to identify and understand the issues that afflict communities, individuals, and the environment. This critical skill is the cornerstone upon which their ventures are built, and it's the catalyst for driving transformative impact.

The Complexity of Social Issues

Social issues are multifaceted and complex. They encompass a broad spectrum of challenges, including poverty, inequality, healthcare disparities, environmental degradation, and more. Understanding these problems requires a holistic perspective, one that considers the historical, cultural, economic, and environmental factors at play.

Identifying Root Causes

Successful social entrepreneurs go beyond surface-level symptoms to identify the root causes of social issues. They ask probing questions, engage with affected communities, and leverage data and research to unravel the underlying factors that perpetuate these problems.

The Process of Problem Identification

1. Research and Data Analysis: The journey begins with a systematic examination of available data, research, and reports. This data provides insights into the scope and severity of an issue. Social entrepreneurs often collaborate with experts, academics, and research institutions to gather comprehensive information.

2. Community Engagement: Effective problem identification involves engaging directly with the communities affected by the issue. Listening to the voices of those who experience the challenges firsthand is invaluable. It not only builds empathy but also reveals nuances and perspectives that data alone may miss.

3. Stakeholder Interviews: Social entrepreneurs reach out to various stakeholders, including government agencies, nonprofits, and existing social enterprises, to gain a comprehensive view of the issue. This can uncover opportunities for collaboration and innovative solutions.

4. Trend Analysis: The examination of societal trends and shifts can be an early indicator of emerging social issues. Social entrepreneurs keep their

finger on the pulse of changing dynamics, enabling them to adapt to evolving challenges.

5. Case Studies and Best Practices: Learning from the experiences of other organizations and social entrepreneurs can provide valuable insights. Case studies and best practices help to refine problem identification and inspire creative solutions.

Uncovering Opportunities for Impact

Identifying social issues is only one side of the coin. Social entrepreneurs are equally adept at spotting opportunities within these challenges. These opportunities often manifest as innovative solutions, business ideas, and ventures aimed at addressing the identified problems.

The Intersection of Passion and Skill

Opportunities for impact arise at the intersection of passion and skill. Social entrepreneurs frequently draw upon their personal experiences, skills, and interests to create solutions that resonate deeply with them. This alignment between what they care about and what they excel at forms the foundation for effective problem-solving.

Creativity and Innovation

Uncovering opportunities for impact involves thinking outside the box. Social entrepreneurs embrace creativity and innovation, looking for novel ways to address social issues. They may draw inspiration from various fields, including technology, design, and business, to develop unique and effective solutions.

A Call to Action

As you navigate through the pages of this guide, remember that the journey of social entrepreneurship is not an academic exercise but a deeply personal and impactful one. Identifying social issues and uncovering opportunities is a call to action, a commitment to making the world a better place.

The following chapters will delve into the practical aspects of creating and implementing solutions, including developing a social enterprise model, securing funding, and measuring impact. Each step in this journey brings us closer to our ultimate goal: creating a world where social issues are not just identified and understood, but actively transformed into opportunities for positive change.

4

Developing Innovative Solutions for Social Impact

I n the previous chapters of "The Social Entrepreneur's Guide to Impact," we delved into the foundational aspects of social entrepreneurship, from understanding its historical evolution to identifying social issues and uncovering opportunities. In Chapter 4, our journey continues as we explore the art of developing innovative solutions to address these challenges and create lasting social impact.

The Creative Spark

Social entrepreneurship thrives on creativity and innovation. It's the ability to think beyond convention and develop novel, effective solutions to complex social problems. The heart of social entrepreneurship is where passion meets ingenuity, and it's here that groundbreaking ideas take shape.

Creativity as a Catalyst

In the realm of social entrepreneurship, creativity is not an optional extra but a catalyst for change. It's the imaginative force that allows you to see possibilities where others see only obstacles. It's the source of inspiration that propels you forward when faced with daunting challenges.

Empathy-Driven Innovation

Empathy is a cornerstone of successful social entrepreneurship. To develop innovative solutions, you must deeply understand the experiences, needs, and aspirations of the individuals and communities affected by the issues you seek to address. Empathy-driven innovation is about walking in the shoes of others, and it's the bedrock upon which effective solutions are built.

The Process of Solution Development

1. Problem Definition: Clearly define the social issue you aim to address. Develop a nuanced understanding of the problem, including its root causes and the challenges it poses. This forms the foundation for your solution.

2. Ideation and Brainstorming: Gather a diverse team of individuals, each bringing their unique perspectives and skills. Engage in ideation and brainstorming sessions to generate a wide range of potential solutions. Encourage open dialogue and creativity.

3. Prototype and Testing: Once you have identified potential solutions, create prototypes or minimum viable products (MVPs) to test your ideas. This iterative process allows you to refine your solution based on real-world feedback.

4. Pilot Programs: Before full-scale implementation, consider launching pilot programs to assess the viability and effectiveness of your solution in a controlled environment. Pilots help uncover unforeseen challenges and validate your approach.

5. Scalability and Sustainability: As your solution proves successful, focus on scalability and sustainability. Develop a clear plan for how your solution can reach a broader audience and maintain its impact over the long term.

Collaborative Innovation

Collaboration is a key element in developing innovative solutions for social impact. Effective social entrepreneurs understand that they don't have to go it alone. They seek partnerships and alliances with experts, organizations, and community members who can contribute their knowledge and resources to the solution development process.

Co-creation with Communities

Engaging with the communities affected by the social issue is not limited to problem identification; it extends to solution development. Co-creation involves working closely with the people you aim to serve, respecting their insights, and valuing their contributions to the development process.

Interdisciplinary Approaches

Innovation often arises at the intersection of different fields and disciplines. Social entrepreneurs embrace interdisciplinary collaboration, drawing inspiration from fields such as technology, design, psychology, and business to create holistic solutions.

Measuring Impact

In the pursuit of developing innovative solutions for social impact, measuring progress is paramount. Effective impact measurement provides clarity on whether your solution is making a difference and guides refinements over time. The process of impact measurement is a crucial aspect of social entrepreneurship and is explored further in subsequent chapters.

The Journey Continues

In the chapters that follow, we will explore the practical aspects of bringing your innovative solutions to life. This includes building a sustainable business model, securing funding, and effectively implementing your solution on a broader scale. As you venture further into your social entrepreneurship journey, remember that innovation is not just a means to an end but a way of life, a mindset that drives positive change and transforms the world one creative solution at a time.

5

Crafting Sustainable Business Models

In the preceding chapters of "The Social Entrepreneur's Guide to Impact," we've journeyed through the history of social entrepreneurship, identified social issues, and explored the process of developing innovative solutions. Now, in Chapter 5, we shift our focus to a critical aspect of your social enterprise: crafting sustainable business models that ensure long-term success while driving positive social change.

The Importance of Sustainability

Sustainability lies at the heart of social entrepreneurship. It's the ability to not only address immediate social issues but to do so in a manner that endures, evolving and expanding its impact over time. Your business model is the blueprint for achieving this sustainability.

Beyond Philanthropy

Unlike traditional non-profit organizations that rely heavily on philanthropic donations, social enterprises aim to be financially self-sustaining. While philanthropy plays a role, it's complemented by revenue generated through the sale of products or services, which are designed to serve a social purpose.

Balancing Profit and Impact

Sustainable business models strike a delicate balance between profitability and social impact. They are designed to generate revenue while ensuring that profits are reinvested in the organization's mission, rather than accumulating for the benefit of shareholders.

Components of a Sustainable Business Model

1. Mission Alignment: The core of your business model must align with your social mission. This alignment should be evident in every aspect of your operations, from product design to marketing.

2. Revenue Generation: Determine how your social enterprise will generate revenue. This could include selling products, offering services, licensing technology, or even generating income through strategic partnerships.

3. Cost Structure: Understand the costs associated with running your enterprise. Effective cost management is essential for sustainability. Consider both fixed and variable costs, and identify opportunities for efficiency.

4. Value Proposition: Clearly define the value you offer to your customers or beneficiaries. This value proposition should align with your social mission and be compelling to your target audience.

5. Customer Segmentation: Identify the specific groups or individuals you aim to serve. Understanding your customer segments helps tailor your products or services to their needs.

6. Distribution Channels: Determine how you will reach your customers. Your distribution channels may include physical stores, online platforms,

partnerships with other organizations, or a combination of methods.

7. Pricing Strategy: Set prices for your products or services that are competitive and fair, while ensuring they generate sufficient revenue to cover costs and support your social mission.

8. Revenue Streams: Identify various revenue streams, which may include one-time sales, subscription models, donations, or grants.

9. Impact Metrics: Develop a system to measure and track the social impact of your enterprise. This data is not only crucial for accountability but can also be used to demonstrate the effectiveness of your mission to potential investors and customers.

Sustainability in Action

Social enterprises come in various shapes and sizes, each with a unique business model designed to support their mission. Consider the following examples:

- Fair Trade Coffee Roaster: A company that sources coffee beans from small-scale farmers in developing countries, paying fair prices for their produce. The business model combines revenue from coffee sales with a commitment to supporting the economic well-being of farming communities.

- Eco-Friendly Fashion Brand: A fashion brand that uses sustainable materials and ethical manufacturing processes. The business model relies on revenue generated from fashion sales, with a portion reinvested in environmental and social initiatives.

- Clean Energy Start-up: A technology company that develops innovative solutions for clean energy production. Its business model involves selling renewable energy systems while reducing greenhouse gas emissions and environmental impact.

The Path Forward

Crafting a sustainable business model for your social enterprise is a pivotal step in your journey. It ensures that your organization can thrive and fulfill its social mission in the long run. In the upcoming chapters, we will explore avenues for securing funding, effective implementation of your business model, and ways to measure and communicate your social impact. As you navigate this terrain, remember that sustainability isn't just about financial stability but about sustaining the positive change you're committed to bringing to the world.

6

Securing Funding for Social Enterprises

In the pages of "The Social Entrepreneur's Guide to Impact," we've covered the foundational aspects of social entrepreneurship, from understanding the historical evolution of the field to developing sustainable business models. In Chapter 6, we delve into a pivotal aspect of your social enterprise's journey: securing the funding necessary to drive your mission and initiatives.

The Funding Landscape for Social Enterprises

The world of social entrepreneurship presents a unique funding landscape. While the traditional sources of capital remain relevant, social enterprises often seek a blend of financial support that aligns with their dual goals of financial sustainability and social impact.

Sources of Funding

1. Bootstrapping: Many social entrepreneurs start with their own savings and resources, dedicating their time and effort to develop and launch their initiatives.

2. Grants and Donations: Foundations, governments, and philanthropic organizations offer grants and donations to support social enterprises. These funds often come with specific requirements or guidelines tied to social impact.

3. Impact Investment: Impact investors, such as impact venture capital firms and impact-focused angel investors, provide capital to social enterprises, expecting both financial returns and measurable social impact.

4. Social Impact Bonds: In some regions, governments and private investors collaborate to fund social programs through social impact bonds. Investors provide upfront capital, and if predefined social outcomes are achieved, they receive a return on their investment.

5. Crowdfunding: Online crowdfunding platforms enable social entrepreneurs to raise funds from a large number of individuals who share their vision. Crowdfunding is a way to generate support and test the market for your initiative.

6. Earned Income: Social enterprises generate revenue by selling products or services that align with their mission. The income earned can be reinvested to further the social impact.

Funding Strategies for Social Entrepreneurs

1. Diversification: Avoid overreliance on a single source of funding. Diversify your funding portfolio to reduce risk and ensure financial sustainability. Combining grants, impact investment, and earned income can be an effective approach.

2. Strategic Partnerships: Collaborate with other organizations, whether they are non-profits, businesses, or governmental agencies, to access resources and funding opportunities. Partnerships can amplify your impact and expand

your network.

3. Impact Measurement: Robust impact measurement and reporting can attract impact investors and philanthropic funders who seek quantifiable results. Demonstrating your social impact is a compelling way to secure funding.

4. Pitching Your Vision: Craft a compelling narrative that communicates both your social mission and the potential for financial sustainability. Effective storytelling can engage potential donors and investors.

5. Build Trust and Relationships: Developing strong relationships with funders, partners, and stakeholders is key to securing long-term support. Building trust takes time but can result in enduring partnerships.

The Role of Impact Investors

Impact investors play a significant role in the funding ecosystem for social enterprises. They seek both financial returns and social impact, aligning with the core objectives of social entrepreneurship. Impact investors range from individual angel investors to specialized impact venture capital firms. Some key points to consider when engaging with impact investors include:

- Clearly Define Your Impact: Impact investors are interested in measurable outcomes. Define your social impact goals and how you plan to achieve them.

- Understand Their Priorities: Different impact investors may have varying priorities. Some may emphasize environmental sustainability, while others focus on community development or social justice.

- Financial Sustainability: Impact investors still expect financial sustainability. Your business model must demonstrate the potential for profitability and growth.

- Alignment of Values: Seek investors who align with your social mission and values. Shared values enhance the partnership and ensure a common understanding of goals.

- Communication and Transparency: Maintain open and transparent communication with your impact investors. Regular reporting on social impact and financial performance is essential.

Navigating the Funding Landscape

Securing funding for your social enterprise is a dynamic journey that requires adaptability and a keen understanding of the funding landscape. In the chapters that follow, we will explore the practical aspects of implementing your social enterprise, measuring and communicating impact, and expanding your reach. As you navigate the funding terrain, remember that it's not just about raising capital; it's about forging partnerships, building a supportive ecosystem, and advancing your mission of creating positive change in the world.

7

Implementing Your Social Enterprise

I n "The Social Entrepreneur's Guide to Impact," we've embarked on a comprehensive journey through the world of social entrepreneurship, from understanding its historical context to securing funding for your initiatives. In Chapter 7, we delve into the practical aspects of implementing your social enterprise, turning your vision into reality, and making a tangible impact on the world.

The Launch Phase

The implementation phase is often referred to as the "launch phase" of your social enterprise. It's the period where you bring your vision to life and start delivering on your social mission. This phase requires careful planning, resource allocation, and a clear execution strategy.

Core Implementation Steps

1. Team Building: As you transition from the planning to the implementation phase, it's essential to assemble a dedicated and skilled team. The right team members should be passionate about your mission and possess the expertise

required to execute your vision.

2. Legal Structure: Ensure that your social enterprise's legal structure is in place, reflecting your mission and allowing you to operate effectively. This may involve registering as a benefit corporation (B Corp) or adopting a different legal structure suitable for your goals.

3. Operational Infrastructure: Establish the operational infrastructure of your enterprise, including facilities, equipment, and technology systems. This is the groundwork that allows your business to function smoothly.

4. Product/Service Development: If you're launching a product or service, devote time to developing it thoroughly. Pay attention to quality, pricing, and any unique features that distinguish your offering in the market.

5. Marketing and Outreach: Create a marketing and outreach strategy to connect with your target audience. Effective marketing not only promotes your offerings but also communicates your social impact mission.

Impact Measurement

Effective impact measurement is integral to the implementation phase. It allows you to assess and communicate the positive change your enterprise is making in the world. Key elements of impact measurement include:

- Defining Impact Metrics: Clearly define the metrics by which you will measure your social impact. These metrics should align with your social mission and be quantifiable.

- Data Collection and Analysis: Collect data on an ongoing basis to track your impact. This may involve surveys, interviews, or the use of technology to gather relevant information.

- Evaluation: Regularly evaluate your impact data to understand trends, areas for improvement, and the overall effectiveness of your initiatives.

- Reporting: Communicate your impact through reports and narratives that resonate with your stakeholders, investors, and customers. Transparency in impact reporting enhances credibility.

Scaling for Greater Impact

As your social enterprise grows and achieves success in the implementation phase, you may consider scaling your operations to have a broader impact. Scaling strategies include:

1. Replication: Expanding your model to serve more communities or regions, replicating the same solution in new locations.

2. Partnerships: Collaborating with other organizations or stakeholders to reach a larger audience and enhance your impact.

3. Technology Integration: Leveraging technology to reach a wider audience, reduce costs, and increase efficiency.

4. Franchising: If your business model is suitable, franchising can be an effective way to scale, allowing others to operate your model under your guidance.

5. Policy Advocacy: Advocating for policy changes at local, national, or international levels to create a broader environment conducive to your mission.

6. Global Expansion: Expanding your impact internationally, serving communities in different countries.

Challenges and Resilience

Implementation is not without challenges. Social entrepreneurs must be prepared to face obstacles and setbacks. Challenges may include financial pressures, regulatory hurdles, and operational complexities. It's important to cultivate resilience and adaptability to navigate these challenges effectively.

Strategies for Resilience

- Continuous Learning: A commitment to lifelong learning helps you adapt to new challenges and stay current in your field.

- Resource Diversification: Building multiple funding sources and partnerships reduces dependency on any single entity.

- Network Building: Cultivate a robust support network of peers, mentors, and advisors who can offer guidance and assistance during difficult times.

- Innovative Problem-Solving: Encourage creative thinking and problem-solving within your team. Solutions often emerge when you approach challenges with a fresh perspective.

The Journey Continues

As you progress through the implementation phase of your social enterprise, remember that this is an ongoing journey, not a destination. The impact you create is a result of consistent effort, a commitment to your mission, and the resilience to overcome challenges. In the chapters that follow, we will explore impact communication, expanding your reach, and the evolving landscape of social entrepreneurship. Each step brings you closer to fulfilling your vision of creating a better world.

8

Communicating Impact and Inspiring Change

I n "The Social Entrepreneur's Guide to Impact," our journey through the world of social entrepreneurship has taken us from understanding the historical context to implementing your social enterprise. In Chapter 8, we explore the critical task of communicating the impact you've achieved and inspiring change in your target audience, stakeholders, and the world at large.

The Power of Impact Communication

Effectively communicating your social enterprise's impact is not just about reporting statistics or data; it's about telling a compelling story that engages, motivates, and resonates with your audience. Impact communication plays a pivotal role in sustaining and growing your social enterprise's influence and reach.

Key Objectives of Impact Communication

1. Transparency: Foster trust and credibility by openly sharing your social impact data and progress.

2. Engagement: Connect with your stakeholders, including investors, customers, partners, and the broader community, to inspire them to join your mission.

3. Advocacy: Mobilize support for your cause, create awareness, and encourage others to take action and address the social issues you're tackling.

4. Sustainability: Secure ongoing support, whether through funding, partnerships, or continued patronage, by showcasing the meaningful change your enterprise is making.

Crafting Impact Narratives

Impact communication often relies on the creation of compelling narratives that bring your impact to life. Effective storytelling is an art that combines data and human experiences to make your impact relatable and inspiring.

Elements of Impact Narratives

1. Human Stories: Share personal stories of individuals or communities directly affected by your initiatives. These stories humanize your impact and show how it changes lives.

2. Data and Evidence: Support your narratives with data, demonstrating the tangible outcomes and progress your enterprise has achieved.

3. Visuals: Use visuals like photos, videos, infographics, and graphics to make your impact more accessible and engaging.

4. Empathy and Connection: Create an emotional connection with your

audience by conveying empathy, passion, and a shared commitment to your mission.

5. Clear Messaging: Keep your messaging clear, concise, and aligned with your organization's values and mission.

Stakeholder Engagement

Engaging with stakeholders is a crucial part of impact communication. Your stakeholders may include customers, investors, employees, partners, and the communities you serve. Engage them in the following ways:

1. Feedback Loops: Establish mechanisms for gathering feedback and input from stakeholders. This not only helps in refining your initiatives but also demonstrates your commitment to involving them in the decision-making process.

2. Collaborative Initiatives: Engage stakeholders in collaborative projects that align with your mission. Partnerships can amplify your impact and garner additional support.

3. Educational Outreach: Conduct educational programs or events that raise awareness about the social issues you address and the solutions you offer.

4. Interactive Platforms: Create opportunities for stakeholders to participate in discussions, forums, or online platforms that allow them to share their thoughts, concerns, and ideas.

5. Employee Engagement: Ensure that your team members are actively engaged and aligned with your mission. Engaged employees are more likely to become advocates for your enterprise.

Impact Reporting

Impact reporting is a structured way of communicating your social enterprise's progress and achievements. Regular impact reports offer transparency and accountability while showcasing the positive change you're creating. Key components of impact reporting include:

- Performance Metrics: Present quantifiable metrics that reflect the progress of your initiatives. Use data to highlight the change you've brought about.

- Narrative Descriptions: Combine data with narratives that convey the stories and experiences of those who have benefited from your initiatives.

- Financial Transparency: Share financial information that demonstrates responsible use of funds, which is crucial for building trust.

- Visual Elements: Use visuals to make your reports more engaging. Charts, graphs, and images can help convey complex data in a digestible format.

Impact Events and Campaigns

Hosting impact events and campaigns is an effective way to engage your audience and create awareness about your initiatives. These events can take various forms, such as conferences, community gatherings, online campaigns, and awareness-raising activities. They are opportunities to showcase your work, share your mission, and inspire others to join your cause.

The Call to Action

As you embrace the role of a communicator in the world of social entrepreneurship, remember that your work extends beyond just your initiatives. It involves inspiring change, mobilizing support, and creating a movement for social impact. In the chapters that follow, we will explore ways to expand your reach, adapt to the evolving landscape of social entrepreneurship, and continue making a difference in the lives of those you serve. Impact communication is not just a reflection of what you've achieved but a catalyst for what you can achieve in the future.

9

Expanding Your Reach and Adapting to Change

I n "The Social Entrepreneur's Guide to Impact," we have journeyed through the diverse facets of social entrepreneurship, from understanding its historical context to communicating impact. In Chapter 9, we explore the crucial topics of expanding your reach and adapting to the evolving landscape of social entrepreneurship.

Expanding Your Reach

Expanding your reach is an essential element of social entrepreneurship, allowing you to extend the positive change you create to more people, communities, and regions. Here, we examine strategies and approaches to scale and broaden the impact of your social enterprise.

Strategies for Expansion

1. Replication: Consider replicating your successful model in new locations. This may involve adapting your approach to suit the specific needs of different

communities.

2. Franchising: If your business model is suitable, franchising can be an effective way to expand. Others can operate your model under your guidance, preserving your mission and values.

3. Partnerships: Collaborate with other organizations or stakeholders to reach a larger audience and enhance your impact. Partnerships can help you leverage resources and expertise.

4. Technology Integration: Leverage technology to reach a broader audience and reduce operational costs. Digital platforms can facilitate online engagement, product delivery, and data management.

5. Global Expansion: If applicable, consider expanding your impact internationally to serve communities in different countries. Adapting your model to diverse cultural contexts may be necessary.

6. Advocacy and Policy Change: Advocate for policy changes at local, national, or international levels to create a broader environment conducive to your mission.

Planning for Growth

Expanding your reach requires thoughtful planning and strategy. Consider the following steps:

- Market Analysis: Assess the demand for your solutions in new markets and regions. Understand the cultural, economic, and regulatory factors that may impact your expansion.

- Operational Scalability: Ensure your operational systems and infrastructure can support growth. Identify areas that may require enhancement to accommodate a larger scale.

- Resource Allocation: Allocate resources efficiently, considering the financial and human resources required for expansion. Develop a budget and funding strategy to support your growth.

- Cultural Sensitivity: Be mindful of cultural differences and community-specific needs. Tailor your approach to respect and accommodate the unique aspects of each community you serve.

Adapting to an Evolving Landscape

The landscape of social entrepreneurship is dynamic, continuously influenced by social, economic, and technological shifts. Adapting to change is not just a necessity; it's an opportunity to remain relevant and innovative. Key aspects of adapting to an evolving landscape include:

1. Continuous Learning: Commit to lifelong learning to stay current in your field. Engage in ongoing education and stay informed about new trends and best practices.

2. Flexibility: Be open to adjusting your strategies and approaches based on new information, feedback, and changing circumstances.

3. Innovation: Encourage innovative thinking within your organization. Explore new ideas, technologies, and approaches to enhance your impact.

4. Environmental and Social Responsibility: Keep a watchful eye on environmental and social issues that may impact your mission. Be prepared to adapt and respond as necessary.

5. Collaboration: Collaborate with other organizations, experts, and stakeholders to stay connected and share knowledge. Joint initiatives can

amplify your impact and contribute to collective efforts to address societal challenges.

6. Regulatory Compliance: Stay informed about regulatory changes that may affect your operations. Ensure that your legal structure and practices are in line with evolving regulations.

7. Scalable Technology: Invest in scalable technology that can support your growth and enhance your efficiency. Digital platforms, data analytics, and communication tools are valuable assets.

Navigating Challenges

While expanding your reach and adapting to change are vital, these processes are not without challenges. Challenges may include resource constraints, increased complexity, cultural differences, and the need for additional expertise. Addressing these challenges may involve:

- Strategic Planning: Develop a clear and comprehensive strategic plan that addresses the specific challenges of your expansion or adaptation efforts.

- Capacity Building: Invest in training and skill development for your team members, ensuring they are equipped to handle new responsibilities and challenges.

- Collaborative Partnerships: Collaborate with organizations that have complementary strengths and resources, reducing the burden of expansion or adaptation.

- Community Engagement: Involve the communities you serve in decision-making and development processes. Engage with local experts and stake-holders to understand their needs and perspectives.

The Ongoing Journey

As you expand your reach and adapt to the evolving landscape of social entrepreneurship, remember that your journey is ongoing. Social entrepreneurship is not a destination but a process of creating lasting change. In the chapters that follow, we will explore emerging trends and opportunities in social entrepreneurship and how you can continue to make a difference in a world that is ever-changing. Your commitment to adapt, grow, and innovate is the hallmark of a true social entrepreneur.

10

The Future of Social Entrepreneurship

As we near the conclusion of "The Social Entrepreneur's Guide to Impact," we turn our attention to the final chapter, where we explore the future of social entrepreneurship. In this chapter, we examine emerging trends and opportunities that will shape the landscape of social entrepreneurship in the years to come.

The Ever-Evolving Landscape

Social entrepreneurship has always been marked by its adaptability and responsiveness to societal challenges. As the world undergoes profound transformations, social entrepreneurship is poised to play an increasingly pivotal role in addressing complex issues.

Key Trends and Opportunities

1. Technology and Innovation: The rapid advancement of technology opens up new possibilities for social entrepreneurship. Innovations in artificial intelligence, blockchain, clean energy, and data analytics offer novel solutions to longstanding problems.

2. Social Impact Bonds: Social impact bonds, which allow public and private investors to fund social programs with a focus on outcomes, are likely to gain more prominence, providing a structured way to address social challenges.

3. Circular Economy: The concept of a circular economy, where resources are used efficiently and waste is minimized, will become integral to social entrepreneurship. Enterprises focused on recycling, upcycling, and waste reduction will emerge.

4. Environmental Sustainability: With the growing urgency of environmental issues, social enterprises focused on climate change mitigation, conservation, and sustainable agriculture will play a significant role.

5. Health and Wellness: As health and wellness gain prominence, social entrepreneurs will address mental health, nutrition, and holistic well-being through innovative approaches.

6. Global Collaboration: Collaboration among social entrepreneurs and organizations across borders will increase, with a shared focus on global challenges such as poverty, healthcare access, and education.

7. Diversity, Equity, and Inclusion: The social entrepreneurship field will place a stronger emphasis on diversity, equity, and inclusion, ensuring that marginalized voices are heard and represented in decision-making processes.

8. Legal Frameworks: Governments and international bodies may further develop legal frameworks that encourage and support social entrepreneurship, offering more favorable incentives and regulations.

Preparing for the Future

To thrive in the evolving landscape of social entrepreneurship, consider the following strategies:

- Foster Innovation: Encourage a culture of innovation within your organization. Be open to new technologies and approaches that can enhance your impact.

- Stay Informed: Continuously educate yourself about emerging trends, challenges, and opportunities in your field. Networking with peers and attending conferences can keep you updated.

- Embrace Collaboration: Collaborate with other organizations and stakeholders. Collective efforts can address complex challenges more effectively.

- Global Perspective: Consider the global implications of your work. Your initiatives may have relevance beyond your local context.

- Ethical Leadership: As a social entrepreneur, lead by example in ethics, transparency, and social responsibility.

- Resilience: Cultivate resilience and adaptability, as challenges and setbacks are inevitable in a dynamic field.

- Impact Measurement: Continue to measure, report, and communicate your impact to attract support and inspire change.

Your Ongoing Journey

The world of social entrepreneurship is one of constant evolution, driven by innovative thinking and a commitment to creating positive change. As you move forward, remember that your journey is not defined by a singular destination but by your enduring dedication to making a difference.

In closing, "The Social Entrepreneur's Guide to Impact" serves as a foundation for your work. By adapting, growing, and continuing to innovate, you contribute to a brighter, more equitable, and sustainable future for all. Your journey is not only a reflection of the world you envision but a testament to the transformative power of social entrepreneurship.

11

The Call to Action

In the concluding chapter of "The Social Entrepreneur's Guide to Impact," we issue a resounding call to action. It's an invitation to embrace your role as a social entrepreneur and to inspire change not only through your work but through your dedication to creating a better world.

The Power of One

The journey of a social entrepreneur is often a solitary one, but it's through the collective power of individuals committed to positive change that we can address the most pressing issues of our time. Every social entrepreneur starts as one, driven by a vision and a passion for making a difference.

The Ripple Effect

Your impact extends far beyond the direct outcomes of your initiatives. Like ripples in a pond, your work inspires change in others. As you lead by example, others take notice and are motivated to join your cause. This ripple effect is a testament to the transformative power of social entrepreneurship.

The Catalyst for Change

As a social entrepreneur, you are a catalyst for change. Your initiatives, your resilience in the face of challenges, and your commitment to a better world all contribute to a broader movement for social impact. You are a trailblazer, illuminating a path for others to follow.

The Challenge and the Opportunity

The challenges facing our world are immense, but they are also opportunities. Social entrepreneurship provides a pathway to address these challenges and turn them into opportunities for positive change. It's a journey that requires determination, innovation, and a belief that, collectively, we can build a more equitable and sustainable world.

The Journey Continues

As you embark on or continue your journey as a social entrepreneur, remember that you are part of a global community of changemakers. Your work matters, your impact is meaningful, and your resilience is inspiring. Embrace the power of your vision and the influence you have to create a more just and sustainable future.

In closing, the call to action is a call to you, to all social entrepreneurs, and to anyone who believes in the potential for positive change. The journey of social entrepreneurship is not one taken alone but is a shared path towards a brighter, more equitable, and sustainable world.

12

Resources for Social Entrepreneurs

In the final chapter of "The Social Entrepreneur's Guide to Impact," we provide a curated list of resources to support and empower social entrepreneurs in their mission to create positive change. These resources encompass a range of tools, organizations, and networks that can aid in your journey as a social entrepreneur.

Organizations and Networks

1. Ashoka: Ashoka is a global network of social entrepreneurs. They offer support, connections, and resources for social entrepreneurs working to address systemic issues.

2. Schwab Foundation for Social Entrepreneurship: This organization works closely with the World Economic Forum and supports leading social entrepreneurs around the world.

3. Skoll Foundation: Skoll Foundation provides funding and resources to social entrepreneurs who are addressing some of the world's most pressing problems.

4. Acumen: Acumen is a non-profit impact investing fund that supports entrepreneurs who are tackling poverty and social issues through innovative solutions.

5. Global Social Entrepreneurship Network (GSEN): GSEN is a global community of support organizations for social entrepreneurs, fostering collaboration and knowledge sharing.

Online Platforms and Tools

6. IDEO.org: IDEO.org provides human-centered design tools and resources to help social entrepreneurs develop innovative solutions that address human needs.

7. B Corp: B Corp is a certification for businesses that meet high social and environmental standards. Becoming a B Corp is a significant step for socially conscious businesses.

8. Coursera: Offers a range of online courses on social entrepreneurship, impact measurement, and related topics from top universities and institutions.

9. LinkedIn for Nonprofits: LinkedIn offers resources and support for social entrepreneurs and non-profits looking to expand their impact through professional networking.

Books and Publications

10. "Lean Impact: How to Innovate for Radically Greater Social Good" by Ann Mei Chang: This book provides insights on applying lean principles to social entrepreneurship for greater impact.

11. "The Blue Sweater: Bridging the Gap Between Rich and Poor in an Interconnected World" by Jacqueline Novogratz: The book offers a

compelling narrative of a social entrepreneur's journey.

12. "Creating a World Without Poverty: Social Business and the Future of Capitalism" by Muhammad Yunus: This book explores the concept of social business and its potential to alleviate poverty.

13. "Measuring and Improving Social Impacts: A Guide for Nonprofits, Companies, and Impact Investors" by Marc J. Epstein and Kristi Yuthas: The book delves into the methodologies of impact measurement.

Impact Measurement and Reporting

14. GIIN's IRIS (Impact Reporting and Investment Standards): IRIS provides a common framework for measuring and reporting impact. It's a valuable tool for impact investors and social entrepreneurs.

15. B Lab's B Impact Assessment: This assessment tool helps organizations measure their impact on workers, community, and the environment, and provides guidance on how to improve.

16. Social Value International: This global network offers resources, training, and guidance on measuring social value and social impact.

Funding and Grants

17. GrantWatch: An online resource that aggregates grants, fellowships, and funding opportunities for non-profits and social enterprises.

18. The Global Innovation Fund: Provides funding to social enterprises and non-profits with innovative solutions to global development challenges.

19. Echoing Green: Offers seed funding and support to emerging leaders with bold ideas for creating lasting social change.

Impact Investment

20. ImpactAssets: ImpactAssets offers impact investment solutions and resources for investors interested in making a difference through their investments.

21. Toniic: A global network of impact investors, Toniic provides opportunities for impact investors to connect and collaborate.

22. Investor's Circle: A network of impact investors, Investor's Circle connects investors with high-potential, social impact enterprises.

Support and Incubation

23. The DO School: The DO School offers a range of programs and innovation labs for social entrepreneurs, providing support and mentoring.

24. Unreasonable Group: Unreasonable Group connects social entrepreneurs with resources, mentorship, and a community of like-minded individuals.

25. Global Accelerator Learning Initiative (GALI): GALI offers resources and data on accelerators and incubators, helping social entrepreneurs make informed decisions.

Legal Resources

26. Legal Structures for Social Enterprises: Seek legal guidance to understand and choose the most suitable legal structure for your social enterprise. Options include Benefit Corporations (B Corps), L3Cs, and more.

The Ongoing Journey

The resources mentioned here are just a starting point. Your journey as a social entrepreneur is ongoing, and you'll continue to discover new tools, networks, and opportunities that support your mission. As you navigate the dynamic landscape of social entrepreneurship, remember that your commitment to creating a positive impact is a powerful force for change. Your work has the potential to transform lives, communities, and the world, one step at a time.

"The Social Entrepreneur's Guide to Impact" takes readers on a comprehensive journey through the world of social entrepreneurship. In twelve chapters, it covers the history, principles, and practical aspects of being a social entrepreneur. The guide emphasizes the importance of addressing social issues with innovative, sustainable business models that balance profitability and social impact.

It highlights the following key themes:

1. Historical Context: The guide starts by exploring the historical evolution of social entrepreneurship, tracing its roots and key milestones.

2. Identifying Social Issues: It then helps readers identify social issues that align with their passions and expertise.

3. Developing Solutions: The guide walks through the process of developing innovative solutions to these social issues and crafting a sustainable business model that supports the mission.

4. Securing Funding: It provides insights into securing funding from various sources, including grants, impact investors, and crowdfunding.

5. Implementing Initiatives: The guide outlines the practical steps of implementing social initiatives, from team building to impact measurement.

6. Scaling Impact: It explores strategies for scaling your initiatives to reach a

broader audience and maximize impact.

7. Impact Communication: The guide emphasizes the importance of effective impact communication through storytelling, data, and engagement with stakeholders.

8. Adapting to Change: It discusses the evolving landscape of social entrepreneurship and the need for adaptability, innovation, and resilience.

9. Resource Support: The final chapter offers a curated list of resources, including organizations, tools, publications, and funding opportunities, to aid social entrepreneurs in their ongoing journey.

Throughout the guide, readers are encouraged to embrace their role as change-makers, take action, and continue their journey of creating positive change in the world. Social entrepreneurship is presented as a dynamic field that offers both challenges and opportunities, with the potential to make a lasting impact on society.